It's all about …

BEASTLY
BUGS

KINGFISHER
NEW YORK

KINGFISHER
LONDON & NEW YORK

Copyright © Macmillan Publishers International Ltd 2016
Published in the United States by Kingfisher,
175 Fifth Ave., New York, NY 10010
Kingfisher is an imprint of Macmillan Children's Books, London

Distributed in the U.S. and Canada by Macmillan,
175 Fifth Ave., New York, NY 10010

Library of Congress Cataloging-in-Publication data
has been applied for.

Series editor: Sarah Snashall
Series design: Little Red Ant
Adapted from an original text by Anita Ganeri and Thea Feldman

ISBN 978-0-7534-7260-6

Kingfisher books are available for special promotions
and premiums. For details contact: Special Markets
Department, Macmillan, 175 Fifth Ave.,
New York, NY 10010.

For more information, please visit
www.kingfisherbooks.com

Printed in China

9 8 7 6 5 4 3 2 1

1TR/1115/WKT/UG/128MA

Picture credits
The Publisher would like to thank the following for permission to reproduce their material.
Top = t; Bottom = b; Center = c; Left = l; Right = r
Cover Shutterstock/ChinKC; Back cover Shutterstock/Vishnevskiy Vasily; Pages 2–3, 4t,
30–31 Shutterstock/QiuJu Song; 4–5 Shutterstock/Kreatif Multimedia; 4l Shutterstock/Henrik Larsson;
4r Shutterstock/Dionisvera; 5tl Shutterstock/HandmadePictures; 5bl Shutterstock/alslutsky;
5tr Shutterstock/kamnuan; 5cr Shutterstock/grafvision; 5br Shutterstock/Vishnevskiy Vasily;
6 Shutterstock/artjazz; 6l Shutterstock/PHOTO FUN; 7 Naturepl/Stephen Dalton; 8 Shutterstock/
Allocricetulus; 9 Shutterstock/Eric Isselee; 10 Flickr/Gilles San Martin; 11t Shutterstock/Bildagentur
Zoonar GmbH; 11b Ardea/John Clegg; 12 Shutterstock/Vasily Vishnevskiy; 13 Shutterstock/Michael
Warwick; 14 Shutterstock/orionmystery; 15t Shutterstock/Cathy Keifer; 15 Flickr/Joshua Byrd;
15b Kingfisher Artbank; 16 Shutterstock/Dimijana; 16t Shutterstock/pan demin; 17 Shutterstock/
Evgeniy Ayupov; 18–19 Kingfisher Artbank; 19t Shutterstock/ M Dykstra; 19b Shutterstock/Cathy
Keifer; 20 Naturepl/Kim Taylor; 21 Shutterstock/orionmystery; 22t Kingfisher Artbank; 22b Naturepl/
Hans Christoph Kappel; 23 Shutterstock/Anton Harder; 24 Shutterstock/Cathy Keifer; 25 FLPA/Erica
Olsen; 25b Shutterstock/Wasan Ritthawon; 26 Shutterstock/reptiles4all; 27t Shutterstock/Tatsiana_S;
27b Shutterstock/Platsee; 28–29 Shutterstock/cyrrpit; 31b Shutterstock/M Dykstra; 32 Shutterstock/
Evgeniy Ayupov.
Cards: Front tl Corbis/Marko König; tr Shutterstock/Suede Chen; bl Shutterstock/Rob Hainer; br
Naturepl/Visuals Unlimited; Back tl Flickr/aaron saguyod; tr Shutterstock/Jan Quist; bl Getty/Ted
Mead; br Shutterstock/chris2766.

Front cover: A Chalcopterus beetle covered in dew drops.

CONTENTS

It's a bug's world!

There is a whole mini world of tiny bugs all around us. There are insects such as ants, wasps, butterflies, and beetles, and other creatures such as spiders, slugs, snails, wood lice, leeches, and centipedes.

grasshopper

ladybug

beetle

Some bugs live on land
and some live in ponds, rivers,
and even in the ocean.

millipede

FACT ...

There are more than one million types of insect.
That's more than any other kind of animal!

bee

butterfly

spider

slug

Bugs all around

Bugs live almost everywhere—in fields, woods, rivers, and towns. Watch butterflies feeding on flowers. Turn over a stone to find a wood louse. See a web outside and you'll know a spider lives nearby.

Earthworms live underground.

SPOTLIGHT: Diving bell spider

Record breaker:	lives underwater
Size:	up to 0.6 in. (15mm)
Lives:	Europe and northern Asia
Eats:	tiny fish and larvae

Insect or spider?

Every insect has six legs and a three-part body. Most insects have wings and can fly.

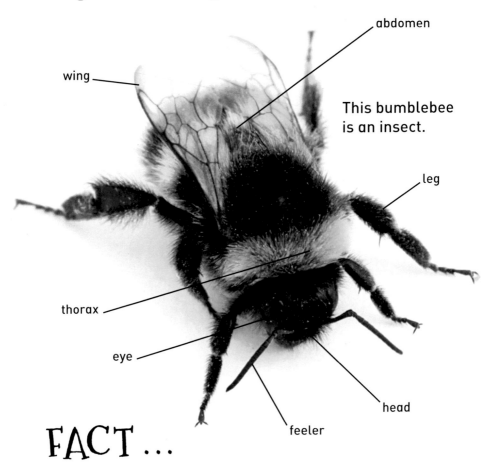

abdomen

wing

This bumblebee is an insect.

leg

thorax

eye

head

feeler

FACT ...

A honeybee flaps its wings about 250 times a second to stay in the air.

A spider has eight legs and a two-part body. Most spiders have eight eyes. Spiders do not have wings.

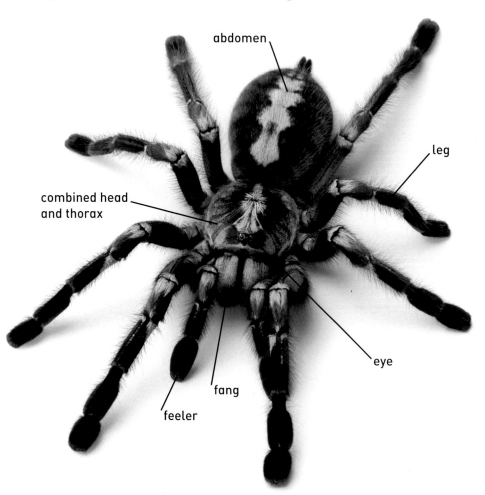

abdomen

leg

combined head and thorax

eye

fang

feeler

FACT ...

A spider can't see very well. It uses the hairs on its body to help it find its way.

Bugs on the move

Bugs move in different ways. Grasshoppers, spittlebugs, fleas, and crickets hop. Slugs and snails slide. Spiders, ants, and cockroaches crawl. Grasshoppers, dragonflies, butterflies, and beetles fly.

FACT ...

Some millipedes have 375 pairs of legs—that's 750 legs altogether!

A grasshopper can jump and fly.

FACT ...

Slugs and snails make a slimy track and then slide along it.

SPOTLIGHT: Spittlebug

Record breaker:	highest jumper for its size
Size:	up to 0.3 in. (7mm)
Lives:	worldwide
Eats:	plant sap

A backswimmer uses its legs to row across the water.

The amazing monarch

Some creatures don't travel very far: they crawl up a plant stem, or fly from tree to tree. This is not the case for monarch butterflies.

In the fall these butterflies fly about 2000 miles (3000 kilometers) from Canada to the warm weather in California or Mexico. In the spring they return to Canada.

Every year millions of globe skimmer dragonflies glide from India to Africa.

FACT ...

Monarch butterflies fly to
the same place every year.
Sometimes they even return
to the same trees.

Bug senses

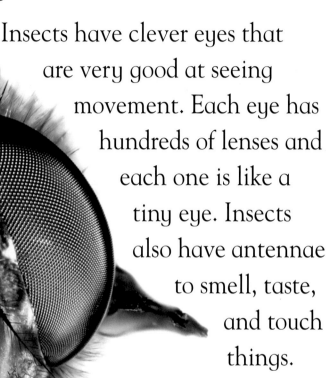

Insects have clever eyes that are very good at seeing movement. Each eye has hundreds of lenses and each one is like a tiny eye. Insects also have antennae to smell, taste, and touch things.

FACT...

A cricket has ears on its front legs.

This male moth has long antennae that look like feathers.

SPOTLIGHT: Dragonfly

Record breaker: most lenses (30,000) per eye
Size: wingspan up to 4.7 in. (120mm)
Lives: worldwide
Eats: small insects

15

Lunchtime

Many bugs eat plants but some eat meat, blood, and each other!

Bees visit flowers to drink nectar and to collect pollen for their young.

A leech sticks onto an animal with its sucker, then starts to drink.

Gardeners love ladybugs because they eat aphids and other pests.

FACT...

Cockroaches aren't picky eaters. They eat almost anything, from plants to the garbage you throw away.

This mantis is eating a spider.

Butterfly life story

Here is the story of how a tiny egg becomes a beautiful butterfly.

In spring, a female butterfly lays some eggs on a leaf.

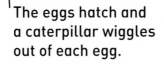

The eggs hatch and a caterpillar wiggles out of each egg.

The caterpillars eat the leaves and grow big and fat.

Each caterpillar makes a hard case, called a chrysalis, around its body.

FACT ...

A female butterfly can lay 100 eggs every day!

18

Inside the case, the caterpillar's body turns into a butterfly.

The chrysalis splits open and the butterfly wiggles out. When its wings have dried in the sun, it flies away.

A butterfly's wings are soft and wet when it comes out of the chrysalis. It waits for the sun to dry them.

19

Good mothers

Most bugs lay eggs then leave them, but there are a few who take care of their eggs.

A mother earwig lays her eggs in a hole in the ground. She keeps them clean and protects them.

female earwig
protecting her eggs

A female wolf spider carries her eggs on her back inside a ball of silk. When the baby spiders hatch, they climb onto their mother's back.

female wolf spider and spiderlings

FACT...

A cuckoo bee doesn't take care of her eggs. She lays them in the nest of another bee.

Bug builders

Some bugs build nests where they lay their eggs. Others build webs and traps to catch food.

Honeybees build a hive in a hole in a tree.

A trapdoor spider waits for its prey in a burrow with a trapdoor.

Record breaker:	builds tallest nests
Size:	0.2 in. (5mm)
Lives:	Australia
Eats:	woody part of plants

FACT ...

Termites build enormous mud nests.
Some termite towers are three times higher
than a tall person.

23

Fangs and stings

All spiders and some insects use venom to kill their prey or to protect themselves.

A spider pierces its prey's skin with its fangs and injects venom.

SPOTLIGHT: European hornet

Record breaker:	largest European wasp
Size:	up to 1.4 in. (35mm)
Lives:	worldwide
Eats:	wasps, large moths, bees

If a wasp is attacked, it can inject venom into its attacker through a long, sharp stinger.

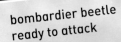
bombardier beetle ready to attack

FACT...

A bombardier beetle shoots a jet of hot poison at its enemies. It fires the venom out of its tail. Bang!

25

Hide and seek

Many bugs use color and pattern to hide from attackers or from their prey. If a small insect lands on this flower, it gets a nasty shock. The flower is really a mantis!

Can you spot the mantis?

FACT ...

A hawk moth has eyes on its wings.
They're not real eyes but they look
scary to birds.

The leaf insect is the same color
as the leaf it lives on.

Hairy monster

Not all bugs are small. The Goliath bird-eating tarantula is the biggest spider in the world. It lives in a burrow and comes out at night to look for food.

The Goliath bird-eating tarantula eats insects, other spiders, lizards, and birds. It waits for them to come close, then attacks.

SPOTLIGHT: Goliath bird-eating tarantula

Record breaker:	world's largest spider
Size:	10 in. (25cm)
Lives:	South America
Eats:	insects, rodents, frogs

FACT...

If a bird-eating spider is scared, it hisses and flicks hairs into its attacker's face.

GLOSSARY

abdomen The back part of an insect's body.

antennae Long thin parts on an insect's head. They are used for smelling, tasting, and touching.

aphid A tiny insect that eats plants.

burrow A hole that an animal digs in the ground to live or lay its eggs in.

centipede A long bug with a lot of body sections and many legs.

chrysalis The hard case that a caterpillar makes around its body.

fang A tooth that squirts poison as it bites.

glide To move through the air without flapping the wings.

hive A nest built by bees.

insect A bug with six legs and a hard case around its body.

leech A bug that drinks the blood of other animals.

lens Clear round parts in an animal's eyes that help it to see.

nectar A sweet liquid inside flowers that many insects drink.

pollen A powder made inside flowers that helps make seeds.

termite A tiny creature that builds huge nests like towers.

thorax The middle part of an insect's body, between the head and the abdomen.

venom A kind of poison that some spiders and snakes make inside their body. They use it to harm or kill other animals.

INDEX